D1806046

INTUITIVE COMPANION

CONSULT YOUR INNER GURU
FOR EVERYDAY GUIDANCE

MICHELE SAMMONS

Intuitive Companion/Michele Sammons — 1st ed.

Paperback: 978-1-7361686-3-9
Hardback: 978-1-7361686-4-6

*Dedicated to those seeking
a consistent and dependable
connection to their intuition.*

Dear Reader,

I truly believe we are born with intuitive abilities—not just some people, but each and every one of us.

Intuition is a natural part of who you are and is designed to be user-friendly and helpful. When your intuition is working effectively, it acts as a light guiding your way forward as you navigate life.

Intuition manifests in various ways, but at its core, it is one true thing—communication from the eternal part of you, the loving Inner Guru You.

If you listen and act on messages from your Inner Guru, your life takes on a magical quality, becoming effortless and fun.

But, it's easy to ignore your intuition because it's subtle. The world's loud distractions and opinions often grab your attention, making it challenging to tune in to the gentle guidance from your Inner Guru.

Without clear communication with your Inner Guru, life feels confusing and complicated.

The Intuitive Companion is a tool that gently guides you back to the subtle energy of your Inner Guru. The loving messages will engage your intuition and inspire your innate wisdom.

As you work with the Intuitive Companion, allow your personal interpretations of the messages to bubble up from within you. Let each message spark deep reflection and unique insight.

Honor your unique way forward by trusting your intuition and your Inner Guru.

With all my love,

Michele

It's important to remember, the *Intuitive Companion* (as magical as it is) is only a tool because you're always in charge of creating your life.

Suggestions on how to use the *Intuitive Companion*:

1. Take a deep breath and allow yourself to come fully into the present moment of here and now.

2. Find your center point—this is the calm, sacred, sweet spot inside you.

3. Without attachment to the outcome, ask your question from your neutral, calm space.

4. Close your eyes. Relax. Let your intuition guide you where to open the book.

5. Place your finger on the open page and read what's there. This is the answer from your Inner Guru. Allow the message to settle into your bones.

6. How does this information apply to your situation? What wisdom is there for you? Reflect on the message and trust that it has meaning for you.

I suggest you honor the evolution of your intuition by using the Intuitive Companion no more than once a day.

BE
TRUE
TO
YOURSELF.

 BE

WHERE

YOU ARE

DIFFERENTLY.

You don't need to understand your Soul's plan for you. You only need to allow it.

The only thing required of you is to take exquisite care of the present moment.

Move forward like you love yourself.

THERE IS NO RUSH.

Your destiny isn't written within the stars. Your destiny is written in your imagination.

Lighten up, Buttercup!

ACCEPT THAT **EVERYTHING** CHANGES.

*You are loved,
supported,
guided,
tended to, and
encouraged
by multitudes
of loving
energy-beings.
Lean on them.*

Your
potential
is...

unlimited.

*Give thanks
for the
goodness on
its way to you.*

You get
what
you give.

RESTORE HARMONY.

EVERYTHING

RESPONDS

POSITIVELY

TO **LOVE.**

Their opinion doesn't matter unless you want it to matter.

You are a miracle worker!

Don't take it personally.

THINGS CHANGE WHEN YOU DO.

GO WITH THE *flow.*

Your joy is the ultimate goal.

Accept.

Accept.

Accept.

Drop the role of victim and regain your power.

FIND

YOUR

CENTER.

Remember your home address is peace. Don't stray too far from home.

There is no wrong choice.

BE BRAVE.

The
Universe
revolves
around
you.

THERE IS
NOTHING
TO BE
AFRAID OF.

Expand
your idea
of what's
possible
for you.

Life is here for your personal entertainment.

WHAT YOU WANT MATTERS SO MUCH.

Surrender
all
resistance.

REACH FOR

RELAXED

HAPPINESS.

Open your heart and take it all in.

Be
happy
in the
meantime.

BEND A LITTLE—

ONE WAY

OR THE

OTHER.

Visionaries illuminate the way forward for others.

You hold a treasure few have ever realized.

DIAL IT BACK.

Focus
on the
journey.

GO
FOR
THE
GOLD.

ALL IS

WELL

WITH YOU.

Your wish is granted.

Don't
sweat
the
small
stuff.

DECIDE NOT TO GIVE UP.

Claim your share of abundance.

A

LITTLE

GOES A

L O N G

WAY.

Be comfortable in your own skin.

Live
today like
it's your
very last.

MAKE FRIENDS WITH THE UNKNOWN FUTURE.

Compliment yourself constantly. You deserve it.

YOU ARE THE MIRACLE.

TRUST THAT THE UNIVERSE WANTS YOU TO HAVE WHAT YOU WANT.

Let your imagination play and it will work for you.

See yourself as
you want to be.

Soon others
will see you
that way too.

Choose
the option
that feels
most
electric
to you.

DO IT ANYWAY.

Don't talk yourself out of making your dreams a reality. You don't know what or who your dreams are for.

Wisdom is gained by those willing to seek it.

PATIENCE

 ## IS

REQUIRED.

START

WHERE

YOU ARE.

START NOW.

Stop entangling with the problem. Set it free.

Be willing to give up the fear to have the fun.

Allow the momentum of the energy to increase before moving forward.

Push the reset button.

YOUR FUTURE IS BRIGHT.

Your work is not to make something happen, but trust that it will.

WANTING TO CONTROL THE OUTCOME IS TRIPPING YOU UP.

STOP
OVER-THINKING.

It all
comes
down to
attitude.

Yours.

Breathe and relax. You are being taken care of.

SHINE

BRIGHTLY

AND

BOLDLY.

Lighten your load.

There is no right way— only your way. You get to pick what that is for you.

START FROM WHERE YOU ARE. IT'S THE ONLY PLACE TO BEGIN.

You are full
of your self!
Beautiful
Life-force
in a body.

Make room in your life for the expansion of energy on its way to you.

You're not meant to see the entire path. Only the next step forward.

Fear doesn't mean wrong direction. Fear means wrong thought about that direction.

THE

UNIVERSE

LOVES YOU.

You are not stuck. At any moment you can choose to create a new experience.

Get on with it.

Source hears you loud and clear.

IT'S TIME.

BREATHE.

_You have been
given many
gifts, talents,
and skills.
Use the ones
that feel good
to you._

Make the best of where you are.

Stop seeking so you can find.

There are places you haven't been where you already belong.

When you
are content
on your path
it doesn't matter
where it leads.

Your Soul is in cahoots with you to make your dreams come true.

Do the strange,
new thing
so that others see
it can be done.

The Universe needs open channels willing to bring new ideas to life.

Stop worrying. It's not the way forward.

Go ahead— amaze yourself!

RESPONSIBILITY IS OVERRATED.

Love with abandon.

You are being taught in Spirit by Spirit.

Anything is possible for you.

SHAKE

IT

OFF.

EXERCISE

YOUR TRUST

MUSCLE.

Be easy about it.

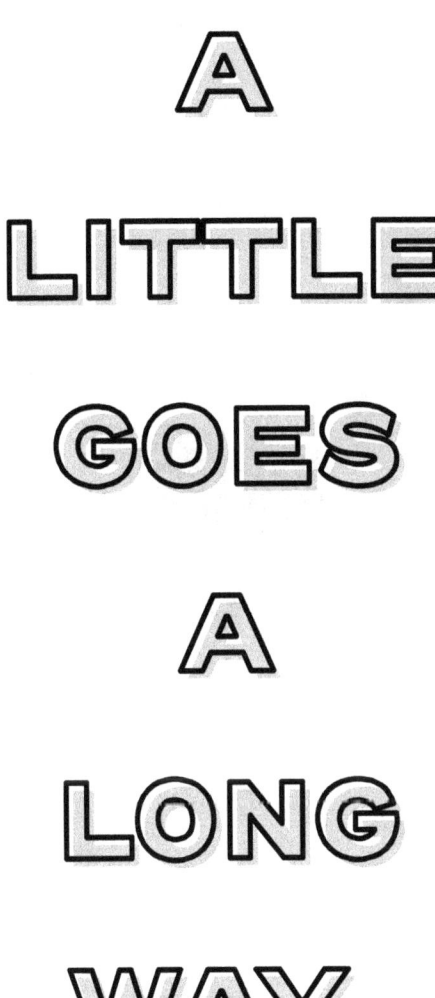

A LITTLE GOES A LONG WAY.

You're already whole.

(Nothing needs fixing.)

The
Universe
will catch
you if
you fall.

YOU ARE

STRONGER

THAN YOU

THINK.

Accept where you are today.

The winds of change are blowing.

NOTHING

REMAINS

THE SAME.

IT WILL BE ALRIGHT.

Some of it's magic. Some of it's tragic. It's all in the way you view it.

Back to the drawing board to reimagine a new future.

True lasting transformation starts on the inside.

FLY YOUR

FREAK FLAG.

You have something beautiful to offer the world.

Trust your excitement to guide you.

YOUR IMAGINATION KNOWS WHAT TO DO NEXT.

Dream yourself AWAKE.

THERE IS NOTHING YOU CANNOT DO.

Forgive yourself and them.

UNLEASH YOUR POTENTIAL!

Seek balance.

LET GO OF

YOUR

SUFFERING.

WHAT YOU

FOCUS

ON YOU

BECOME.

When you make excuses, you're stalling.

The light
in you
recognizes
the light
in them.

NOW IS
THE TIME.

Surrender to the will of the Divine within you.

Give up all
claims to
punishment.

YOU

ALREADY

KNOW THE

ANSWER.

Listen to your heart's intelligence.

WELLNESS IS THE ORDER OF THE DAY.

You
are
healed.

STAND

IN YOUR

POWER.

Trust the process. It's working its magic on you.

It's okay to change the rules when the old ones are broken.

YOU
GOT
THIS!

SAVOR MORE.
FIX LESS.

LOVE
is the
only
answer.

Find what feels good.

THERE ARE NO MISTAKES. ONLY CLARIFYING POINTS FOR WHAT IS NEXT.

The only
permission
you need
is your
own.

*Gather yourself.
Spreading your
energy too thin
helps no one—
especially you.*

Living in your head keeps you from living in your heart.

TINY BABY STEPS

COUNT AS

PROGRESS.

Make the best of it.

You are safe.

*There is plenty
to go around.
All you have to
do is let it in.*

Be the light that illuminates the dark spaces.

YOU

PLEASE

SOURCE.

TIME TO PUSH THE P A U S E BUTTON.

Your happiness or sadness affects the entire Cosmos.

SOURCE IS ESPECIALLY FOND OF YOU.

RELIEF IS A SIGN YOU'RE MOVING IN A BETTER DIRECTION.

All
problems
resolve
themselves.

SEE ONLY WHAT YOU WANT TO SEE.

YOUR JOY IS HIGHLY CONTAGIOUS. SPREAD IT AROUND.

Money is a flow of energy. It flows in and it flows out.

Dream more.

Effort less.

IS IT FUN? BECAUSE THAT'S THE ADVENTURE YOU SIGNED UP FOR.

LET YOUR HAPPINESS MANIFEST IN ANY WAY IT WANTS TO APPEAR.

Surrender

your doubt.

If you're waiting for the other shoe to drop, you can stop worrying. There is no other shoe.

What you want
and what you fear
are only thoughts.

Think more about
one than the other.

The Universe has already said YES. Begin to look for evidence of this.

Loving
thoughts
create
a loving
world.

THE STUFF
YOU DON'T
LIKE IS
HELPING
YOU TOO.

Experiencing transformation is not always easy, but it is oh so worth it.

*There is
no good reason
to hide
your bright
beautiful light.*

You are
more powerful
than you are
choosing to
believe.

Long ago a seed was planted inside of you.

YOUR GENTLENESS IS YOUR STRENGTH.

IT'S OKAY TO REST.

Source is
standing
right next
to you.

Their attention to you or lack thereof, speaks more about them than you.

Trust Yourself!

The Best is yet to come!

CPSIA information can be obtained
at www.ICGtesting.com
Printed in the USA
LVHW081955270921
698842LV00002B/109